Somewhere in Ecclesiastes

The Devins Award for Poetry

Somewhere in Ecclesiastes is the 1991 winner of the Devins Award for Poetry, an annual award originally made possible by the generosity of Dr. and Mrs. A. Devins of Kansas City, Missouri. Dr. Devins was president of the Kansas City Jewish Community Center and a patron of the Center's American Poets Series. Since the death of Dr. Devins in 1974, his son, Dr. George Devins, has continued to sponsor the award.

Somewhere in ECCLESIASTES

Poems
by
Judson Mitcham

Judson Mitcham

Bread Loaf, 1992

University of Missouri Press
Columbia and London

Copyright © 1991 by Judson Mitcham
University of Missouri Press, Columbia, Missouri 65201
Printed and bound in the United States of America
All rights reserved
5   4   3   2   1   95   94   93   92   91

Library of Congress Cataloging-in-Publication Data

Mitcham, Judson.
  Somewhere in Ecclesiastes : poems / by Judson Mitcham.
    p.   cm.
  ISBN 0-8262-0802-9. — ISBN 0-8262-0803-7 (pbk.)
  I. Title.
PS3563.I7356S66   1991
811'.54—dc20   91-22821
                                                        CIP

♾™ This paper meets the minimum requirements of
the American National Standard for Permanence of Paper
for Printed Library Materials, Z39.48, 1984.

Designer: Rhonda Gibson
Typesetter: Connell-Zeko Type & Graphics
Printer: Thomson-Shore, Inc.
Binder: Thomson-Shore, Inc.
Typeface: Trump Mediaeval

For my mother and in memory of my father

. . . but time and chance happeneth to them all.
—Ecclesiastes 9:11

Contents

Acknowledgments

The author wishes to express his appreciation to the National Endowment for the Arts, which provided financial support for the composition of these poems through a Creative Writing Fellowship.

Poems in this volume, or versions of them, first appeared in the following: "On the Otis Redding Bridge," *Antioch Review*; "Night Ride, 1965," *Black Warrior Review*; "Sunday Evenings," *Devil's Millhopper*; "About Women," "Epistles," "In the Kingdom of the Air," "A Knowledge of Water," "Laments," "Nature," "Notes for a Prayer in June," "Somewhere in Ecclesiastes," "Surviving in Tolstoy's Dream," and "Where We Are," *Georgia Review*; "Driving Home from the Clinic" and "Explanations," *Gettysburg Review*; "Playground in the Rain," *Ironwood*; "Last Words," *New England Review*; "The Touch," *Poetry Miscellany*; "Rocking Anna to Sleep," *Poetry Northwest*; "What You Have Need Of," *Prairie Schooner*; "Loss of Power," *Southern Poetry Review*; "Home," *Tendril*.

"Explanations" was reprinted in *The Pushcart Prize XIV: Best of the Small Presses* (Pushcart Press, 1989). "Wonder" appeared, along with some of the poems listed above, in *Notes for a Prayer in June*, a limited edition chapbook (State Street Press, 1986).

Somewhere in Ecclesiastes

Notes for a Prayer in June

1

        The other boys lived,
and a prayer grew from this:
the unbelievable sadness of chance
and the shattering dazzle of glass still strewn,
days later, on the road.

2

My son won't let things go, and I love
his fighting to understand, in his own terms.
Having learned about light years, he recalled
the distance to the school, how heavy
his legs felt when he raced there.
        What form
will his knowledge of the wreck take,
when he learns how, late one Sunday,
twenty Junes ago now, I flung you from the world,
through a windshield?
        Will I tell him
how I ran to get help,
yet tired, had to slow down, my legs turned to lead,
had to rest in the face of death, how far
I have traveled through the years?

3

I remember the late spring night we camped out
on Alcovy Mountain, just the three of us
who later on would take that ride.
We laughed at ourselves for playing war.
We were nearly sixteen.

And it seems like a last act of childhood,
crawling up the north slope
so softly I could reach for a branch,
draw a bead down its gnarled barrel
and laugh you dead.
                        The next morning
when absolute darkness had failed, for a while,
we stood without words above the world,
a white mist drifting far beneath us
forever, over homes we were headed for.

4

Is it breath rising in the Christmas air
as a child pedals up and down the driveway at dawn?
Is it dizziness with which
a woman has to reach for the words
to send into silence with her son?
                        Each June,
it's the brief taste of salt, licked away,
as a boy hurries out to the street, having breezed
through the hot kitchen, kissed his mother's face.

5

Before our eyes, that heavy old coin disappears,
while it stays where it is. We're aware
sundown is a lie now,
though we see it the same. Chimpanzees
pause, sometimes, from their foraging or play,
sit quietly and gaze into the west
until moved by darkness.
                        Perhaps, in their eyes,

nothing seems magical, or it all does. From us
comes a forced, final nod toward the sleight
of relentless method, how it turns
pure mystery to laughter in the end.
                                        Still,
we know there's a magic we begin with, tricked
by love's act into this ruled world.

                              —for Glenn Hawkins, Jr.

Wonder

It can start with nearly anything, the delicate theme
of a late-night talk show or the desperate, false
laugh track of a bad sitcom. Sometimes,
I see us all sitting here
lulled off forever by a gas leak, and the TV
still selling us deodorants and beer, selling lies
about our lives. I want to turn
from the dead screen able to say
this life is a holiness, it is all we will have.
I want to load us into an Oldsmobile
with windows that won't roll up, upholstery
musty from years in the garage. I want to ride,
washed with the summer air's warm velvet cloth,
ride to where the stars come clear, where the road
goes from blacktop to concrete slab, sudden dirt.
I want to trouble dust for miles, till we roll
to a hill overlooking a farm,
where a long gold light floats out in a field
like a lost ray of sun, where the cattle lie buoyed
by the earth, their heavy spines curving over hearts
slowing in the drift toward sleep. I want to feel
how the old car trembles and dances and kicks,
trying not to die, then click the lights off,
kill the engine, and listen
to the tree frog, cricket, and cicada staccato,
the soft lows rising, as in wonder, from the darkness,
as if asking, repeatedly, *What are you doing here?*
Why are you here?

The Touch

—for my mother

You stepped out the back door, drying your hands
on a plain white apron
and watching me slap the new basketball down
on the driveway's nearly flat hardpan,
unable to control it or to stall,
for long, its falling still.

You held out clean, wrinkled hands for the ball,
let it drop and caught the rise
with the fingertips, never with the palm,
allowing no sound but the ball's hollow bounce,
crouching low, either small hand
moving *with* the ball.
                              And years later,
when the Newton County Rams came down,
like the cavalry at dawn on a few Cheyenne,
in a hot-breath man-to-man press, the best plan
was to get the ball to me. Even now,
I return to that late fall morning
when you taught me what a softer touch could do,

how to go where I needed to, never looking down.

Laments

For a Small Boy Confused about Words

What country are these folks from, you wonder,
who follow the machine-gun nonsense
the man on the truck bed talks, these folks
who are whispering words you know,
like *whiskey* and *pity* and *wife*.
                              But how
can a man really drink away a farm?
You imagine the fish pond tilted like a cup,
all the cows guzzled dry,
the milk barn, farmhouse, miles of barbed wire,
and the John Deere melting like a sliver of ice
on the highway's soft tar in August.
                              Nothing
remains unswallowed but the sky
which surrounds you now, wherever you stand,
like a glass turned upside down.

For a Man Who Carries His Lover's Baby Picture in His Wallet

You follow the full moon home, so empty
you ease off onto the shoulder
of the shortcut you always take, cut the engine

and listen to the hot block tick
like a heart too irregular to live with.
Again, you look at the snapshot

you carry for her mouth, the trace of icing
on the lower lip slightly pushed forward, as if
she begins just then to be sad. And it hurts

that the baby's not looking at the camera,
that the beautiful, Bible-dark eyes gaze off,
forever, past the one who is holding her.

For an Old Man Who Can't Remember His Mother's Face

Your left breast pocket's still vivid with its medal
of day-old egg, and your pants
sag like a clown's flowered trousers, or those

of a man living alone, no woman to reflect on,
with something like cancer—but it's not that—
eating his weight. You shuffle to a seat

in the corner, by the last snooker table
at Freddy Bray's shotgun pool room.
A fight kicks up without warning. A cue stick

kisses your cheek in a backswing, leaves you
lapping up the powdery dust, the crisp hulls
of insects swept to the wall. You know

she expects you to come straight home after school.
She's forgotten what it was to be a girl, all day
ironing in other folks' homes. You can feel

her hands moving over your clothes, making sure
the creases are sharp when you start out. Now,
you struggle up onto your feet, and you think

of her eyes when she sees this blood on your shirt.

Rocking Anna to Sleep

It was almost sorrow, what I used to know
as a child, not wanting to drift off,
hearing the even, deep breaths
of my brother, to whom
everything was lost: the cracked door's
line of pure light climbing the wall,
far down Church Street, a solitary bark
catching on, even the cool pillow,
its familiar smell.
                        The small breaths
of the girl failing in my arms
grow slower and deep.
She trails this worn blue nylon nightgown
all over the house. She loves
the feel of one button. But I know
if I lifted her hand,
it would easily open and fall back
free as a raindrop.
                        The rocker's soft
creak keeps time. I let it die.
And perhaps she's startled by the change
or has gone so far in her dreams,
she can say—by tightening her grip
when I pull at the gown—*you are wrong
if you think there is nothing in the world
you can always hold.*

Epistles

Dear Solomon: Her father got drunk, then he came
to her room.
It grew like hatred inside. She would dream
of a monster with a face nearly hers,
its acid tongue licking at tissues
close to the heart.
                                She awoke
to the round, old faces of forgotten dolls
still lined on her shelf,
some with hollow eyes, unraveled smiles;
others stayed whole, their blue eyes wide,
as though they were waiting, amazed,
to see what she would do.
                                One day,
she tore them all in half,
sat crying and rocking for a long time,
as she cradled those small, wrong bodies in her arms.

———————————

Dear Salome: Remember what Nietzsche said?
A day in which one has not danced
at least once seems wasted. When he wrote this,
he remained alone in his cold room,
while his mind stepped out, trying to charm
the universe back to his flat.
                                On the street
in Turin where he broke down,
perhaps dreaming of a girl's slender waist,
he embraced the smooth neck
of a horse being flogged. In the years to come
he would circle through the cramped attic rooms
of his mother's house

and quickly pass mirrors, where a head
had a mad stare after that wild dance.

———————————

Dear Jesus: But what if, against all odds,
Hitler is found,
alive but not well in Atlanta, his mind
not demonic but childlike, so his hours are spent
cutting roads through oatmeal, cuddling a rag doll
he was given by the Salvation Army, and he thinks
the memories are really bad dreams, a breast
stretched into a lampshade, ornately carved
crosses and combs wrought from bone, all things
human redeemed?

Night Ride, 1965

Exactly at one o'clock,
I crawl out, walk the half mile to the dirt road,
wait for the loud DeSoto, its gold now sanded dull brown,
color of damp pine straw. When the car slows,
dust catches up, steams forward through the headlights,
into the dark. The farm station signed off for hours,
all the others too remote for the aerial,
the radio's faint rasped harmony's lost
to the car's bass throb. As we cross the main road,
we can look down at the small town's single row of stores,
streetlights blazing like a runway
only the desperate or crazed would try to land on,
and we cruise all night down narrow county roads,
talking as though we could say it all, could tell
what it means to grow quiet at the first light,
while the stars all fail, what it means
finally to turn home
with the clear crackle of tires rising from the wet road,
as sweet cut fields come cool through rolled-down windows.

On the Otis Redding Bridge

—Macon, Georgia

This morning, when a woman walks home
from the graveyard shift at the cotton mill;
when she comes to the Otis Redding Bridge, coughing,

and turning her head, so the snowflake dust
on her shirt whirls off through a sheer gold sleeve
the early sun lays across the road,
                                        what I need
is the voice of Otis Redding —

and the power that would let a man shout
sanctified, tender, and sad, let him cry,
angry, yet shocking in his praise.
                                    I want to sing
the cotton dust caught in the sunlight;
and the woman who is not slowed down in the least
by the momentary beauty that began

as an old pain deep in her lungs; this woman
who spits off the bridge and goes on.

Surviving in Tolstoy's Dream

He tacks past the desk, smelling foul, like spoiled onion,
and, as always, of alcohol. What he wants
since winter turned hard weeks back,
he finds right here—a place to sit where it's warm,
a bathroom anyone can use, clean water,
a trash can next to a vending machine
in the basement, and more. Other bums don't make it.
Bones wanting softness, they will flop onto sofas
which line the walls holding current magazines,
leafing through what they have grabbed, maybe *Life*,
Ebony, or *Better Homes and Gardens*. In a wink,
mouths fall slack, hands surrender, and the slick
picture books slip from their laps.
No sleeping allowed, they are ushered out.
But the man I follow, looking up from the cards,
veers toward someplace else. I would bet
his story is flawed by a flatness inside,
by the rambling, sad chapters on job, wife and blood,
jail and children, alley and rain. I have seen
how bare his eyes are, no different from the others',
as if burned clean of memory by enough
alcohol or scoured of what they've known
by a wind which returns any dawn, eager to pin
trash like last week's classifieds against
a sharp ledge or a charged fence. When he limps
from the last rank of fiction,
he takes off his camouflage Army coat, carefully
lays it over the back of a straight chair
at the table he's chosen, then frees three buttons
of his outer shirt, peels off a layer of flannel,

jabs shirttails into bottle-smooth corduroys, walks
to a fountain on the far wall, guarding his book
like a full pint of Thunderbird, something which no one
would leave unattended. When he sits, grandly,
as if coming to a fine, free meal, he cracks the novel
to its heart, starts to read, lips moving, and as easily
as swilling any day's first drink, enters the dream.

Home

The TV's white noise
hisses me back, this first
awareness the worst one: lights on,
wine by the bed, stale cigarettes,
chicken box greasy on the Gideon,
an hour before dawn. The orange moon
on the far wall's dull watercolor
is nowhere in the lake.

I remember my father's game.
Having come from the mill,
settled in his chair, he would say
"There is something odd in the room."
Unseen, either he had hidden
something in plain sight,
pencil in a flower pot,
or changed things slightly,
setting the clock back
or taking a knob off the radio.
He knew how simple it was
and watched us, giving no clue.

When the trucker overhead slams home,
his kicked-in turquoise door
not catching, the chain on mine
rattles. I recall
there was never a prize back then.
There was only the seeing.

Playground in the Rain

The rain falls hard, straight as chains
the worn, still swing seats hang on,
and the slide flares darkly, its blade
clattering as though each sound it has known
could return—each loose, ticking shoestring,
every open coat rapping metal buttons,
a buckle or a zipper. In the hollows
by the seesaw, underneath the swings, in the bare
circle at the jungle gym, puddles form.
The horses have lost their eyes to the weather,
waiting in a perfect line. Their guts
give a thick, dark coil to the mud.

I think of how things go wrong,
how Janice Scott suddenly dropped limp
through a tangle of bars, how the seesaw
caught Leon Dillard under the chin,
shattered his jaw, broke teeth. And I think
of a boy we had cruelly called Baby Shoes because
he was small for the first grade,
who meandered in the path of a swing, as it arced
backwards as far as it could, then rode
the weight of a large child down to his temple.
I recall how the blood made beads in the dirt,
the children all gathered as quietly as clouds,
and the playground grew this still.
                                        I recall
how differently everything gleamed, as in rain,
the paths home, curves in the bars, those shoes.

In the Kingdom of the Air

By now, everyone knows there is nothing
in everything.
How easily we see it
in the old man dragged by a self-propelled mower through his
    yard,
in a cloudy winter noon when a single leaf waves at the sun,
in the first quick smacks of the rain.
Maybe,
a thousand miles from anyone who loves you,
you encounter some woman who has stolen the face
of your mother, and she hurries on by.
I have stood
in the dark near a window
of a tall office building while a couple made love on a roof
several stories beneath. I could see
every privacy, the way
she twisted her mouth, how he fumbled and rushed,
then wrapped her in the blanket they had laid across the tar.

We have all seen a child's blue balloon floating low
and ghostly in the hall, losing helium.

But a woman turns sharply through an intersection.
The back door opens, and her two-year-old falls beneath the
    wheels
of the next car through. Who will fail
to inhabit that woman
as she drives away, completely unaware;
as she pulls down the visor, then frowns, realizing
she forgot to buy the milk; as she notices
the headlights flashing behind her?
Who,
turning, doesn't gather up the air, doesn't enter
the kingdom of the air?

Somewhere in Ecclesiastes

The one who will not contend with realities gets phantoms to battle against.

—Kierkegaard

1. Accident

A kitten, startled onto the stove, tips over
a pan of boiling water.
And a little boy, weakened by his burns, must surrender

to pneumonia, must become
a piece of deep blue in the puzzle
his mother hasn't yet put together. He is sky,

surely, but the kitten—what is it?
A diagonal of rain? Does she have to fit it in—
the streak of soft gray? Who will tell her?

Her friends have faith in mysterious ways.
They say it, and they say it, until God
himself kicks the handle of the pan. And for her,

all the colors turn ugly and cruel unless
there is chaos at the root of every beauty—she is wild,
remembering his eyes—and we are blessed

only by accident, only by chance.

2. Soul

What if it were true, after all,
that the body is a garment, a light cotton shirt
we will easily do without?

If we knew this beyond any question,
would it alter the funerals of children?

                              Imagine
a world in which the mother of a seven-year-old
who was killed in a wreck doesn't come
from the new grave feeling like a woman

who struggles up out of a lake, soaked,
wearing everything she owns,
and who can't take anything off, not a scarf,
not a ludicrous hat with a feather.

                              What
if the body were a silk slip lifted in the hands
of a lover, then tossed on the floor,
with a laugh?

3. *Man*

While the dust rolls in from the road, he remains
by the open front door of the gas station,
sitting on a turned-up Coca Cola crate,

as though he has been there forever, as though
there is no other home he can go to.

If you gesture, headed for the door, he will nod,
slightly, in return. He will raise one hand
to his greasy red baseball cap, whose bill
is pulled down low, so he has to lean back
to look you in the eye, if he chooses to.

He chain-smokes cigarettes, dropping the butts
in the two long swallows of beer grown hot
in the bottle at his feet. He imagines
the back of your neck in the cross hairs
as you walk toward your car; or he thinks

of calling out "Wait"—then telling, again,
if he can, what happened to his son.

You have seen this man. He appears,
like the dust caught loitering in air by the late
afternoon sun, anywhere.

4. Son

This is all routine,
but I can't stop watching you and taking in details:
the first, barely visible growth
of fine, dark hair on your upper lip;

your lanky frame's angles, revealed
by the one thin sheet; the foot sticking out
with a half-moon callus on its ball;
and the profile—flattened at the nose, badly broken
just a few hours back by an elbow.

You don't even flinch when the nurse
jabs in the needle, but it leaves me thinking
of a morning last week when I saw
a yellow jacket writhing in a shroud, caught
by a spider which had climbed on its victim
and was thrusting in its poison. I remember

that the rhythm seemed to build to a shudder
as the spider pulled away;
the yellow jacket's panic disappeared, so he lay
in his silver-white hammock of silk, rocked
by the breeze. And your eyes glaze over. I am sure

this is all routine: the curtains have begun
to shimmer like the fall sun glancing off water;
and now, when I try to hold your hand,
you shake me off and smile, tiredly, going under.

5. Heaven

Heaven is a ghost town. No one remains
where the road dead-ends into desert. At noon,

rattlesnakes cool their skins in the dark
lobby of the old hotel. A letter
yellowed in a drawer says "Everyone's fine,
and the good Lord willing . . ." then it blurs.

There's a baby doll swaddled in cobwebs
on a board rotting through in the mercantile,
a cry still poised in its throat. *Mama*

is the word it will call only once
if the shelf lets go. The weather-vaned roof
of the one-room school's fallen in. The whine
of the wind turns mockingly human.

6. Morning

When I walked out back with my coffee
to investigate a large red flower
sprouting in the uncut grass, I discovered

it was really two tall spider lilies
whose blossoms were entangled,
they had grown so close. Reaching under,

I broke one stem, and its bloom
hung cradled in the petals of the other.

And soon after dawn this morning,
a neighbor's cat bent to a pothole
in the driveway. A pale blue shimmered

in the puddle's black sheen, as the cat
glanced over at the rustle of my paper.
She held my eyes for a while,

then turned back, slowly, to the hole
and lowered her mouth to the sky.

7. *Sun*

To sleep late, eat a light breakfast, and step,
leisurely, into the sun;

to smooth on coconut oil and recline
on a soft, thick towel, then cultivate the calm
simplicity of the gulls
that sail down low over the wet, glassy sand,
undisturbed by their reflections.

                             Later on,
to drink a little wine and eat a sandwich
in the room. Though it's cool,
to turn the air high, then ease in under
the covers. Reaching over to the nightstand
for the Gideon, to let it fall open, at random,
somewhere in Ecclesiastes,
                       and to sleep.

To wear a white Panama hat on the beach
and a painful new skin. To be finishing
a paperback mystery greasy with oil,
a deeply flawed novel, still compelling
with unexplained death.

There is a time to heal, and a time to cast away,
to turn each page with an absolute faith.

8. Rain

When the long drought broke, we sat on the front porch,
  watching
in silence, as if
it were any other rain, while the sheets of dark silver
  hissed down
on the hot blacktop.
We could smell the rain washing through the corn, ten acres
of dwarfed brown stalks we would soon plow under.

When we all ate supper at my uncle's house,
my great grandmother had forgotten, again,
her own son's name. The simplest things—
utensils and napkins, the passing of bowls—
easily confused and defeated her.

But my grandfather told us a story:
when Jack's Creek flooded years ago,
a Guernsey had swum, unharmed, all the way
down to Highway 11, then strolled into town—
as haughty as Geraldine Phillips, he said,
and snorting when it walked, just as she did.

Hearing that comparison, my grandfather's mother
started laughing. She cackled so intensely
her upper plate floated in her mouth, nearly clattered to the
  table,
and her pale skin reddened, and she rocked, shaking hard,
till her son had to take her in his arms.

We had all gone limp in our straight chairs, wiping back
  tears,
when she quit, falling quiet once again. And we sat
listening to the rain.

9. Poem

I'm seduced by a poem that can move
like a beautiful woman,
sultry in her black silk dress. She will step

through the soft, golden lighting of a restaurant,
assuming she has lowered our voices—and she has—
as we follow her return from the ladies' room.
She is elegance and style
                                          until she whirls,
discovering a light green, three-foot banner
of toilet paper trailing from her right high heel.

But I am searching for a poem that redeems
like an elderly widow
living in the country by herself. She's aware

of every little sound; she is frightened by the wind
cutting through a locked screen door, by the hoot
of an owl, too deliberate and low. Every night,
she will lay a small pistol and a dog-eared Bible
by her pillow, just to feel

the smooth, empty chamber of his favorite, to inhale
the tobacco in the paper, and to fear
nothing she remembers then, and nothing she can hear.

10. Design

The swallows wheel off through the aisles, as if
they are set free here,
within this design. I have always loved

the strict, dark geometry of pecan groves,
those cathedrals of shade:
the clean, hushed acres of shadow, the cool

avenues of dusk,
the bare, neural branches in the late fall
reaching through the fog, or as though

delicately traced, in India ink,
on the shadings of red in a sunset.
And the small, quick flocks of the swallows—

I have loved those too, how they move
beneath one skin
the color of the breeze, with only one thought

rising when they billow and fall. And tonight,
they have spiraled all over the grove.
They have settled in the matrix of trees, as if

euphoric, released, all talking at once.

Explanations

A boy holds a blown-glass sparrow in his hand
and can't resist testing one finger against
a clear, fragile wing. When it gives,
the child looks up at his mother. As if
to revise what has happened, he explains:
he didn't press hard enough to snap it. The crippled
figure is to blame.

And when Nietzsche went insane,
when he buried his bushy face deep in the neck
of a horse whipped hard in the street, of course
there was someone to haul out the photograph
of Nietzsche himself hitched up to a cart
driven by the woman he had loved, the young
Salome wielding a whip.

I remember
Jesus' explanation to his puzzled disciples
of his speaking in parables. Otherwise, he said,
the heathen would understand too, and they
would also be saved. I have always believed
Jesus had a zany sense of humor.

Consider
the way we are taught and defeated, at once,
when a thought angles back on itself,
as when Plato alleges that Socrates lies
with every single word from his mouth, and then
Socrates owns up, holding, with a smile,
that Plato has spoken the truth.

I recall
my son and his best friend, each one lost
in his own loud monologue, rolling their battered
matchbox cars down the driveway.
My son said, "History can start any time."

And his friend fell silent, appearing to ponder
how history is born,

then shook his head yes,
as though he had understood fires and freak wrecks,
leukemia and early, slow death well enough
to start off walking down the hill, not saying
just anything he happened to think of.

About Women

Who is more foolish than the poor man
who tries to give his son the honest truth
about women?
           When the boy is thirteen,
the man thinks back to how the world had to change,
how its giving curves began to fill him up,
and he wants to tell his son what it is
he has learned since then, what women
might mean in his life.

So he tells the boy Paul was surely wrong
when he said to the Corinthians
if a man could get by, not touching a woman,
that was good. He relates how Freud
died, still baffled by females. He pulls in
Darwin to explain why everyone turns
to watch a certain girl walk by.
                       And he talks
of Saturday mornings, when the sun slants in
through the bedroom window,
how his wife comes warm into his arms
to share the way the dust luxuriates in light,
to lie there and listen to the house as it settles,
to the rustling of children in the next room,
and to drift back, together.
                  But he thinks
of something he will keep to himself:
his desire for a woman at the beach last year.
She was old, slightly bent, not beautiful.
Her housedress trailed through the foam, gaped open

to the waist.
                    He is puzzled, uneasy,
remembering his daughter
in the mornings, how he finds her, tightly curled,
shivering, the quilt kicked off. How she wakes
facing any wall, turned at random, as if spun
like a bottle, unaware, though she has dreamed.

What You Have Need Of

Again, the stars gathered like children at dark
into light, taken like the clearest of dreams
into quiet, yet there, you are gone.

Once, the old *World Book* still tucked under your arm,
you led me into a field, away from the lights of houses,
to show how the whole figures are not there,
and therefore, you draw your own lines, how then
you can link what's scattered into anything.

And what you have need of flares in that far
eternity that dies too, quiet village of the universe.

Tonight, when sleep, failing, has fallen into old grief,
I have walked out into the back yard, hearing that voice,
and waited where the land slopes downward miles
to the town's lights, a clear lake raised to the stars,
darkness floating on the far last ripple of streetlights.

There are those who defeat their dreams, who know,
when the brother of childhood stands in the doorway,
not to believe, but I am not one.

Where We Are

Coals raked out on hearthstones writhe like men.
Lake weeds resemble a madonna, and great rocks
erode into profiles, smiling at clown-faced clouds
or frowning, puzzled as they peer far down
at long-dry stream beds, unable to find old light.
Blossom, starfish, mandrake, shadows in snow
open their arms. Everywhere, eyes spiral:
in the leaves of water lilies they are amazed,
in slow creeks' vortices sleepy, a little sad,
in wood grain knowing, nearly sensual, in wings
of hawkmoths, blind. And hands are found in coral,
ears in shells, the small breasts of young girls
in tree trunks, skulls in walnuts. But faces
draw us as though we were infants: to chrysalids
swaying on the underside of leaves, to sawn marble
and photos of the surface of Mars, to ice melting
an old man into the wind, to hollow, dead trees
and shacks blank-eyed on hills. There is also Christ
burned into hearths, into cloth, photographed
in thunderstorms, forest fires, waterfalls, and found
gentle in walls, the torn asbestos of a henhouse,
lichen of cathedrals.   But this is not enough.
There's the taste of dust churned up from a dirt road
a wrecked pickup has rattled down, late summer,
the dusk like cooling iced tea, almost too sweet,
and the truck's wake coaxing a crushed wing upward.
There is rippling lake light slowing, how blackbirds
coil far off like smoke, shadows of small clouds
sailing in the fields. Always, there is rain,
its slow coming on in a heavy, ticking stillness,
how it sounds on the old barn's dark tin roof
or dripping from trees afterwards, when steam

curves ghostly along the blacktop, and new skies
gather in puddles. There are paths followed
at dawn through grazed fields flaming with dew,
the paths worn smooth as the handles of old tools.
And fireflies floating through the night, brief smells
of plowed earth caught through diesel, or colors
of sundown fallen in the hills, the cool air
sharpened with coal smoke, dark coming early,
when something is found.

Nature

. . . we, who are last year's dust and rain. . . .
                              —Loren Eiseley

1

Men of science knew it in their bones, that if light
travels at the speed of God, only one thing
in the universe could match it—

a human thought shooting through the nerves.
But who could get a reading? The velocity
easily would equal that of starlight.
                                        Yet,
when Helmholtz measured the speed
of the impulse, he chuckled. Even though
the metaphor remains *illumination*, we're aware

an idea arrives like a child
who plays hard all afternoon, self-involved,
who somersaults off across the yard, who discovers

it's dark before he knows it.

2

There's a yellow moon low over the parking lot.

My son, seventeen, points it out
as we slam the trunk shut on the groceries,
"Look at that."

We have held off work all day.
He played my old guitar, I read a novel,
and we have driven to the supermarket, set

to bring home only the necessities.
We stand here taking in the moon
through the earth's dusty lens, and I resist

giving anything but "yeah" as an answer.
When he holds out a hand for the keys, chooses
a longer route back to the house

and rolls too slowly down Maplewood Lane,
once nearly coming to a stop, he does not
explain. The yellow moon

follows us, whichever way we turn.

3

Maybe I am simply tired out by the drive,

but far up in the bleachers, when I hear
the high school's valedictorian
quoting Emerson,

if I let myself go, I could cry. A light breeze
sweeps through the humid June dusk. A woman
in the next row whispers, then returns

her attention to the amplified words.
But the wind picks up, until it billows
through the boy's purple gown, until he seems

an adolescent Moses, come to lead
his people to the wilderness, his voice
cutting like the scripture,

quoting Emerson. There is
the wind and how it sounds, like distant thunder,
blowing on the open microphone. Then there is

the thunder in the distance, and the difference.

4

We had to get a loan to cut it down.

Drought took several years to kill it, but then
limbs began to plummet
to the roof from a hundred feet up. Mr. Brown,

in the business all his life, gave his word
he had never cut a tree this big, then he wrote
an estimate far below the others.

He worked two days, with a crew of ten men,
on the red oak older than the country,
and he left the ground level. It was late

on the second afternoon when a few of those men
visited the truck for a pint of Old Crow.
The oak itself offered up the smell

of a strong, honeyed wine gone sour in the cask—
centuries of rain, the men agreed,
had fermented in the wood. And when they left,

we kept on standing in the yard, challenged
by the air, as if something
essential still needed to be done, but we

were only human.

Driving Home from the Clinic

On the narrow back road to Monroe, after rain,
the air was a bittersweet tea
of mayweed mixed with the creek, wild onion, and pine,
the freshly turned earth like a root split open,
then held to the nose.

I drove home slowly, with the windows rolled down,
and I listened to the hush of the tires
on the damp asphalt,
felt the patches of cool air washing my arm,

saw a farmhouse lighted by a single yellow bulb
and drifting far out in a field
as dark as the bottom of a lake, while the clouds
to the southeast blossomed with lightning.
                                        God,
it was all of this, even
the smell of a polecat killed on the road
mingled with the wild sweet olive, this
and the news,
that compelled me to know, for the first time,

that I want to grow old,
to entertain grandchildren, telling true stories
that surprise them at the end,
stories of things long past, yet to happen.
To be able to say:

The night it all started, there was jasmine
floating on the air.
There was mica in the wet road, glistening. Cicadas
had remembered how to sing.

A Knowledge of Water

I love the way the cows go down to the water
and wade in deep, till the nostrils rest
on the pond's copper film. In July,
when the oak shade bakes like a shut loft,
all the cattle walk off into coolness, feel
their heavy meat lift.
                                    So the body
they drink from consumes them, becomes
a eucharist busy with flies. This stink
of pond slime, piss, and rotting possum
swallows till their giant taw eyes
gaze across the surface, where the light
changes every move.
                                    And I believe
they can nearly take it in, like a drink—
the ripple, slope, fence, pines, sky—
and they walk from the pond onto earth
with a knowledge they will bear,
crossing dry pastures at dusk, single file,
their wet flesh heavier than before.

Loss of Power

The noon news chokes off, war in a man's throat.
The fan's blade quietly spins to a stop.
The bulb over a full sink fails. All this
happens at once, and a child shouts
"Hey" from the next room, comes
running to a man who is not surprised,
but oddly shocked, at the loss.
                            A mill worker,
a laid-off doffer in the card room who worked
sixteen hours routinely, he looks up
powerless to change this, and he thinks,
for the first time in his life, of the shape
the .38 would make in his pocket,
and that no one would know him far away,
at a small bank in Ellijay
or a liquor store in Hartwell.
                            But tonight,
when his wife has laid out her tips on the steps,
far short of what Georgia Power wants,
he only walks, hands in his pockets, to the mill,
where he leans his forehead on the warm brick,
placing his palms on the trembling wall, feels
the power work through him like prayer.
For a long time, he stands like this.

Sunday Evenings

Sunday mornings seemed wrong for the soul,
so fragrant and perfect were the worshipers,
like a garden club arrangement of rare bulbs.
What I wanted was a field at dusk,
with dandelions leaning in the breeze.

In the evening there were always those
grown wildly alone. When Raymond
turned slowly into the aisle, leaned
doubled on his cane, unable to go on;
when Billy Reed's mother,
a sad, bent woman
who had gone so far into silence, sang,

then the world's true music touched ours,
all the windows of the old church open in June
to the mournful barks, fast whispers of tires.

The Beginning of Heaven

I have dreamed three times of my father
in the year since he died, yet twice he remained
faceless as a shadow:
having struggled from his bed,
he embraced me and vanished through a door;
and he waited like a beggar on the steps—
this was Thanksgiving night—but disappeared
when he tried to give his name.
                                    Maybe dreams
were the origin of heaven:
say a man came back as himself,
not an actor in the theater of grief,
but the actual man, with his laughter, his walk;
unmistakably, his hands.
                                    Close to dawn,
my father leaned back from the front seat,
holding three wrinkled five-dollar bills,
one for each child, and when his eyes—
absolutely his—grew amused
as we grabbed for the money; when he turned
and cleared his throat once, like a man
prepared to force everyone to listen,
but then simply reached for the key,

I believed we'd continue up the drive,
we'd complete that half-mile ride to the fair,
the giant wheel visible, already, where we were.

Last Words

An old woman stands at the casket.
"Don't he look natural?" she asks.
I think about the phrase "of natural causes,"

how it indicates a different kind of violence.
I do know what she means,
and both of us admire the awful craft

of the worst undertaking in the world,
the taking under.
She turns from his petrified face. Raised

on her tiptoes, she whispers in my ear,
"I thought so much of your daddy." Odd,
I didn't really think of him at all,

or so it seems, now
that he's a riot in my head.
And everything he gave me,

which was everything he had,
I took that as a given. Only Saturday,
we talked on the telephone a while, but I can't

remember what he said.

Sunday

1

With six young blacks at the door of the church,
suddenly, in 1963,
and the preacher out of town, the decision
fell to you, as the chairman of the deacons.

You took them down the aisle, and I recall
you put them on the left, second pew,
in the same place Ben and I had waited,
at ages three and four, for the anthem
to be over. You would come down from the choir
to sit between us then.
                              I couldn't quit
glancing at the visitors,
who gave away nothing, not a trace
of the strain they must have felt.
                              That Sunday,
across the kitchen table, we agreed,
intensely, on the clarity of scripture:
"My house shall be a house of prayer . . .
all ye who labor and are heavy laden . . .
knock, and it shall be opened."

The congregation voted two to one
only one week later to exclude
Negroes from the services,
                              and soon—
confused by many things I couldn't name—
I would find this hypocrisy convenient
as the reason I would leave the Baptist church
or any other faith. I made you pay
for staying on. What did I desire?

A man in a signboard trumpeting "Repent"
on the corner of the all-white church? Perhaps.
But I made this judgment from the sofa,
while watching old movies on the TV,
                                    reading
the fat Sunday paper,
starting with the comics and the sports.

                        2

A Sunday is a parable of time, always was.

In the hard-shell old days,
you couldn't drag a stick across the dirt.
The stick became a plow, the mark a furrow.

We heard those stories from your mother,
having traveled to her house after church, to sit,
forever, in the parlor, underneath
the portrait of a stern young man
at the center of the mantel.
                        Legend had it
dancing got him turned out of the church.
Your father, in his coffin twenty years
when I was born, loved the mandolin
and the banjo that could bring him to his feet.

I like to think of that. And of the Sundays
when men played semipro ball on the mill field,
doubleheaders stretching into dusk,
into chimes coming soft over the pines, *sweet hour
of prayer.*
                Best of all, I remember

a pitcher with a slowness close to magical—
knuckleball, palm ball, sinker,
butterflies he fluttered at the batter.
                                        Back then,
following the evening benediction,
often we would drive through the center of Monroe—
ghostly in its calm—
to the only place open, the Trailways station,
for the ice cream cones we had to eat

strategically and fast, that sweetness which began
melting as we took it in our hands.

                        3

This is partly explained, I am told, by the tricky
physiology of shock:
                        I reacted
as though I had heard good news—a bizarre
confusion on a day of great clarity, with each
blossom of wild red clover, every breath
and bony arm sharply redefined. I had heard
my brother say thickly,
"He's gone."
                        There are those
who insist the word *love* explains nothing,
but is only a maneuver, like music, in the effort
to follow what the body figures out. Who has not
believed each move of a dream

till instructed by his name, or the daybreak? Who,
having reached my age, hasn't once
grown silent while the talk trickled on, got a look

at the faces of bone, then turned
with an ache to say it all?
                              Here's a story
I'd forgotten: early August in the Philippines, you
with CQ duty, while your buddies trucked off
to the show. Kay Kyser, at the close,
had stood with his arms wide, sobbing, to announce
it was over.
              So the men came back
dancing in the street, some choking out prayers
or running just to run, others quieter than ever,
observing themselves, oddly frightened.
                              When Ben
telephoned the news,
euphoria appalled me, joy washed over
my body. I'm unable to explain. I'd believe,
if I could, in the shock of sudden victory.
                              The only
word I have is *love.*

                              4

A sophomore stuffed with philosophy,
                              home
from college on the weekends,
I cultivated arguments with you, attempts to show
the doubtful ontology of heaven.
Not arguments exactly—I would lecture, and you
would sit there listening, at times
asking me a question.
                      When the honeymoon
of grief left off, when I quit
letting go on the back road, headed for work,

or waking in the night, on my feet,
as if the telephone had rung,
                              I discovered
anger like a child's pure fury
at a simple recognition—the authority, say,
of gravity or sleep.
                              I am kneeling
at the grave, with a butcher knife in hand,
hacking at the dark fist of ice
that won't turn loose of the yellow silk flowers
we buried in the vase last summer.

Finally, it splits. Lynda kneels
with the bright poinsettia for the cylinder.

When you came to get us up, Sunday mornings,
for a few years there—it became a family joke—
you did it on cue:

the Lefevres sang "*I'll* fly away . . ." signing off
a half hour of gospel on the radio. Why
do I think about this, still gripping the knife,

having nothing else to hit, with such a purpose?

                              5

Instead of heading home, one Sunday at noon,
we turned up 138, and we stopped
at a family place, east of Conyers.

But Mama didn't really have an appetite. To me,
it was army food—greasy, mass-produced.

The restaurant was hot, the lighting harsh,
the tables too close, and the single price high.

I took her to the other side of town,
to the small monastery she had never seen,
and neither had I, in the early afternoon,
when the sun angled down through the windows,
indigo and gold on the chapel floor.

A man walked alone through the sanctuary,
never looking up.
                              On the road
to Monroe, fields of goldenrod flickered
in the wind. When I wondered out loud
about the name of that weed,
she told me what it was, without surprise.

And I think about a morning at the old house,
of you and me looking at a spider web
delicate with light.
I reached out to tear the thing down,
and you caught me by the wrist.
                              If I believe
it was not a bright pain
that made your eyes open on a Sunday
in April, who will stop me? If I name

the day itself, the day of rest, the dust,

the silver-white filaments of dust floating down,
slowly, like a dream of falling snow,
through the avenue of light by the bed.
                              If I say
it was this that took your breath.